You Made Me Late Again!

PAM AYRES

You Made Me Late Again!

MY NEW COLLECTION

EBURY
PRESS

1 3 5 7 9 10 8 6 4 2

First published in 2013 by Ebury Press, an imprint of Ebury Publishing
A Random House Group company

Copyright © Pam Ayres 2013

Illustrations copyright © Susan Hellard 2013

The Random House Group Limited Reg. No. 954009

Addresses for companies within the Random House Group can be
found at www.randomhouse.co.uk

A CIP catalogue record for this book is available
from the British Library

The Random House Group Limited supports the Forest Stewardship
Council® (FSC®), the leading international forest-certification
organisation. Our books carrying the FSC label are printed
on FSC®-certified paper. FSC is the only forest-certification
scheme supported by the leading environmental organisations, including
Greenpeace. Our paper procurement policy can be found at
www.randomhouse.co.uk/environment

Printed and bound in Great Britain by Clays Ltd, St Ives PLC

ISBN 9780091940461

To buy books by your favourite authors and register for offers visit
www.randomhouse.co.uk

Contents

∾

Introduction

I first discovered that I liked writing when I was a pupil at the Church of England primary school in the village of Stanford in the Vale, then in Berkshire.

In 1952 at the age of five, I trooped into this building for the first time, along with a crowd of other reluctant scholars from the swathes of children who would come to be known as the baby boomers.

The school, in a somewhat mean-spirited fashion, had windows placed far above our heads so that no fascinating event taking place outside on the street would ever distract us from the task in hand. A herd of cattle passing at milking time or the annual arrival of a moth-eaten funfair went unseen. We might have heard the sounds if, as we sat at our ink-stained desks, the teacher had tugged on the lengthy cords and opened the windows a crack. Otherwise, we gazed at the cream-painted walls.

Over time, these walls were regularly adorned with my own work. I could spell, I liked learning new words and I found I could write stories. The teacher read these out to the rest of the class and pinned them on the wall. This did little to ensure my popularity with other pupils, but coming as I did from a jam-packed council house where the priority of my exhausted mother had to be grub and plenty of it, the attention was nice.

I did not start writing verse until I was about twelve. I wrote parodies of the then-popular Lonnie Donegan songs, and I used it to try to get a laugh from my friends, writing about their clothes, make-up or first hesitant romances. It didn't always work and more than once they walked off when I was still in mid-flow. This was disconcerting when I had spent hours crafting the masterpiece, but not a bad preparation for life as a performer.

I started performing my verses and songs round the folk clubs in the 1970s. These places were a godsend to me because they provided a performing space although you lived out in the sticks. Most pubs had a folk club night with a friendly audience, and these were a priceless training ground where you could make ghastly mistakes and kindly friends would gloss over the embarrassing bits and congratulate you on the parts that worked. Here I became a paid performer for the first time, earning £12 for a twenty-minute session of songs and poetic efforts. I was more thrilled than I can ever express to be selling my own work and hearing people laugh. Unbeknown to me, a group of entertainers soon to become household names were also working the folk clubs in their own areas at that time. Billy Connolly, Jasper Carrott, Mike Harding and Max Boyce benefited from them as I did. The folk clubs were like the comedy clubs are today. They enabled you to take a deep breath, summon your courage, get out there and give it your best shot. They saved me from my typist's life, which I hated.

I know that many people, sometimes those you would least expect, enjoy writing funny poems and verse. It is a popular pastime and people often ask me how they can progress with their work. I can only tell them what I did. I was fortunate to come to the notice of BBC Radio Oxford, who gave me a weekly spot, and I was also immensely lucky that when I printed a little pamphlet of my poems and tried, with knocking knees, to sell them to local bookshops, nobody was scornful or showed me the door.

I think it's important to write about things which people can identify with. I wouldn't recommend any subject too rarified, or anything concerning people you know but other people don't, because then your readers feel excluded. I don't think it matters how ordinary the subject is, as long as you approach it from an original angle.

Words have such a fascinating rhythm within themselves, so that in one, the stress is on the first syllable and in another, it is on the last. This can be harnessed to make a marvellous bouncing tune, and the more words known and understood, the richer the finished effort.

Here is a collection of pieces I have written over the past few years. These include poems, verses, tweets, anecdotes and sketches. They cover a wide range of subjects from a nervous racehorse afraid of running in the Grand National, to the proud reflections of a new granny, and from a dog reunited with his master at the Pearly Gates to the regrets of a woman who last night danced too long and too hard and now can't stagger across the kitchen.

I hope you like them and that they brighten your day a

little. Thank you for buying this and my previous books. Thank you for enabling me to spend so many happy years putting it all together.

Pam Ayres, July 2013

My friend invited me to her sixtieth birthday party, but I didn't really want to go. This didn't reflect my feelings towards my friend, only the fact that I'm not usually keen on parties and feel perfectly happy at home. It's the idea of getting dressed up in some uncomfortable frock and tottering off in high heels, the prospect of a lot of people talking at once, the crush, the hours of standing, the alcohol-fuelled cheerfulness that depresses me. I'm the life and soul of any party.

I went, of course. I'm very fond of my friend and as is so often the case when you are not looking forward to an event, it turned out to be a total triumph. On that most perfect mild evening, the guests were riveting, the food sumptuous and what a band! Mike d'Abo's group had been booked; they were sensational. Having matched their music perfectly to the occasion, they had all the sixty-somethings rocking to Rolling Stones numbers: 'Jumpin' Jack Flash', '(I Can't Get No) Satisfaction', 'Honky Tonk Women'. I rocked with the best of them, I gave it everything I had and more. That night I felt as fit as a fiddle, on top of the world, bursting with energy. I danced and danced. After a time my husband sloped off, so then I danced with anyone who asked me, and when they stopped asking me I danced with my handbag. It was a magnificent, exhilarating night when I really could have danced until the dawn.

However in the morning, things were not quite as good ...

The Broken Woman

Last night we went out to a party,
We decided, we were dressed, and we were gone,
It was only up the road at Roy and Brenda's,
We were in a party mood so *bring it on!*
And though the bloke who played the keyboard
   started sagging,
Though the vocalist was ashen with fatigue,
Still on the floor, the pair of us were dancing,
Endurance? There was no one in our league!

When we got up to do 'The Locomotion',
There was no one there could say we'd lost the knack,
But this morning as I try to cross the landing,
I feel as if I might have broke me back,
Or it could be more a fracture of the pelvis,
I can get about, I'm all right once I start,
But I have to shuffle very, very slowly,
And keep me legs about three feet apart.

The addicts they were clustered in the garden,
Lighting up their fags and their cigars,
It was probably a clear and perfect evening,
But the smoke was blocking out the moon and stars,
They had a fella there just like Sinatra,
I shouted, 'Turn the music up, let's hear him *sing!*'
But frankly, I am coming to regret that,
This morning I can't hear a bloody thing.

I never liked that niece of Roy and Brenda's,
But later on, when we were sitting down,
I think I might have told her all my secrets,
And this morning they'll be all across the town.
I felt exuberant! I felt amusing!
Fascinatingly high-spirited and young!
For the music had released my inhibitions,
And the alcohol had loosened up my tongue.

When the band had packed their gear into the Transit,
And the cats were on the wreckage of the feast,
We staggered up our road on Sunday morning,
And the sun was slowly rising in the east.
I don't know what was in that last libation,
I laughed fit to bust at everything I saw,
Only now I can't remember what was funny,
And I feel as if I might have broke me jaw.

My shoes are lying shattered on the carpet,
Where I kicked them off with loathing and relief.
They were new at the beginning of the evening,
Now I look at them with utter disbelief,
With bloodshot eyes I turn them in my fingers,
One night was all it took to wear them out!
In the bin they go on Sunday morning,
Never more to do the 'Twist and Shout'.

So far no encounters with my husband,
Since we came singing up the stairs at half past four,
I couldn't say I'm feeling optimistic,
There's groaning from behind the bathroom door.
Last night I was soaring like an eagle,
But like Icarus, I flew too near the sun,
So this morning I am just a broken woman
Devastated that my dancing days are done.

*F*or some years now we have had a small herd of Dexter cattle. Though they are very characterful and nice, it's always wise to be careful around them because it is frighteningly easy to get hurt. This is not so much because one of the animals takes a sudden dislike to you, more that one further back in the crowd takes a dislike to her neighbour. She bunts the neighbour, the neighbour cannons into the one you're talking to, and you in turn are unceremoniously flattened ...

I Was Standing by the Cow

I was standing by the cow, who was standing by
    the cow,
Who was standing by a cow who got annoyed,
For gentle summer zephyrs,
Had unsettled all the heifers,
And they ran around the pasture overjoyed.

But the cow by which I stood, wasn't feeling
    very good,
She was out of sorts and disinclined to play,
It was rather pitiful,
She had hoped to meet the bull,
But the blighter turned and walked the other way.

Well, it made the others laugh, but she
    hankered for a calf,
And would make a perfect mother she was sure,
A little calf in sweet repose,
With a pink and shiny nose,
A version of herself in miniature.

Well, they had a bull named Floyd, he just stood
   there unemployed,
Or would feign a sudden interest in a star.
And the cow, whose name was Nancy,
Had quite failed to take his fancy,
And he walked off saying, 'La di da di dar.'

So she gave him such a bunt, struck him squarely in
   the front,
He was wearing an expression of surprise,
A domino effect resulted,
In that Floyd was catapulted,
And his whole life slowly passed before his eyes.

I was standing by the cow, who was standing by
   the cow,
Who was standing by the cow who got annoyed,
The flowers were sweet, the bees were humming,
And I never saw him coming,
I was flattened by a fat and flying Floyd.

So by way of chain reaction, I have both my legs
   in traction,
And I watch the daily setting of the sun,
So if the cow by which you labour,
Has a mind to bunt its neighbour,
Do not stand on ceremony – run!

A Patient's Prayer

O Lord I pray on bended knee,
Defend me in the A & E,
So if a bed costs too much lolly,
Grant at least a porter's trolley.

W hen I was a young woman, I used to think that romance was exclusively for young people. The idea that older people might have feelings of that sort was rather unsavoury to me – not quite nice, a little distasteful.

Well, I don't feel like that now. However old we are, I don't believe we ever lose that dream of the perfect partner, the soul mate, the one and only. In fact, I suspect a large percentage of women go through life still secretly waiting for the man they <u>should have been with</u>.

I was telling an audience about this theory once, and a man at the back shouted out, 'Yeah, that cuts both ways and all!'

I Still Haven't Given Up Hope

℘

I still haven't given up hope you know, I still await
the day,
When my true romantic hero comes to carry me away,
Well I've been married thirty years, some people
find that long,
But my husband's just a stop-gap till the real one
comes along.

Then, like Lawrence of Arabia across the burning sand,
I see him ride towards me and I take his
outstretched hand,
I see his pearly teeth, the flash of sunlight on enamel,
And if love cannot sustain us, we shall have to eat
the camel.

You Made Me Late Again!

Well done. You've made me late *again!*
You know I'm not one to complain,
But all my careful plans have gone to pot.
Yes, you can make a face and groan,
But if I'd been on my own,
I guarantee I'd be there *on the dot.*

We're in the rush hour, *thanks to you*,
I can't *think* what it is you do,
That makes us late in every situation.
We could have *sailed* there, calm and sweet,
But now there's gridlock on the street,
And we're staring at our watches in frustration.

Oh God, they're all out here today,
Shift over Grandpa! Out the way!
Overtake or let ME have a chance!
Oh, make your mind up sunshine, do!
He's got a *monumental* queue,
The poor old geezer's driving in a trance!

Are you not warmly dressed or what?
Because this car's so bloody hot!
It's boiling! It's like crossing the equator!
Could you not turn it down, *my sweet*,
Before I pass out from the heat,
Which of course would make us even *later*.

D'you really need the radio on?
Because my concentration's gone,
Don't say you're going to eat *another* snack,
And must you sit there like the Queen,
With that infernal magazine?
You're blocking out the mirror! Oh, SIT BACK!

At last we stop, and as we park,
We see the house is cold and dark,
Our friends abandoned hope and went to bed,
Now, as if things could not be worse,
We face the journey in reverse,
If only we had left home *when I SAID!*

But at this point, his gracious wife,
Who'd endured him all her life,
Ordered up a taxi on her phone,
Then, with her finest leather boots,
Kicked him firmly in the glutes,
And went to live contented, on her own.

The Animal Shelter at Gardners Lane

There are rabbits and guinea pigs, fancy and plain,
At the animal shelter in Gardners Lane,
Terriers eager to sniff out a rat,
Puppies who long for a cuddle and pat,
Older dogs, portly and easy to tire,
Who dream of a basket up close to the fire,
Gerbils and hamsters, downcast and forlorn,
And floppy-eared rabbits to nibble the lawn.

Here are beautiful creatures to suit every taste,
Lovable animals going to waste,
Cats of all colours, the modest, the vain,
Who had a home once and would like one again.
But family circumstance blows them off course,
Through ignorance, cruelty, death and divorce,
No longer required, left out in the rain,
They come to the shelter in Gardners Lane.

Here they are welcomed and vetted and fed,
With a kind friendly voice and a comforting bed,
And the breakfast's on time, and the brush and the comb,
And the walk in the grounds. But it isn't a *home*.
A place to belong; they would love it so much.
A basket, an armchair, a garden or hutch,
It's what they all dream of and hope to attain,
At the animal shelter in Gardners Lane.

So at night, when the darkness is studded with stars,
Please remember the faces that look through the bars.

A Dog at Home

I always like a dog at home,
It makes it nice and hairy,
And if a burglar calls,
Your dog will make the place sound scary,
Your dog will idolise you,
And his love will never stop,
You only need some food and drink,
A bucket and a mop.

Insomnia

I just can't get to sleep tonight, no matter what I do,
I'm restless in our bed, I fuss and fidget next to you,
I rather think the reason is, I fell into the trap,
Of having quite a heavy lunch and then *a little nap!*

It wasn't very long, a little doze, the way you do,
And no way was it longer than about an hour. Or two.

And then, when I woke up, well it was suppertime
   you see,
I did eat quite a lot again, between you and me,
I rather overdid it and I dined just like a toff,
And watching television later on ... I nodded off.

It wasn't very long, a little fade, a little snooze
My eyes were closed ... but I was concentrating on
   the news!

My husband doesn't understand my trials, which is hard,
He has a low, sarcastic nature, which I try to disregard,
He recommends a remedy to overcome my plight,
Stay awake by day and only go to sleep at night.

I take a short siesta! Nothing lengthy whatsoever,
Fifteen minutes maximum. *(Observes husband, off stage
  right)* Oh was it? Well, whatever.

It's a dreadful thing, insomnia, I suffer every night,
The time goes by so slowly when you're waiting for
   the light,
I went to see the doctor to discover what he thinks,
But sitting in the waiting room, I did have forty winks.

It wasn't very long and it was over in a flash,
I woke up leaning heavily on someone with a rash.

Alas the doctor had no cure, prescription or appliance,
It's clearly a condition quite unknown to modern science,
Experts are exasperated, quailing at the quest.
I'm such an enigmatic case … I think I need a rest.

If I could only sleep illuminated by the moon
As readily as I achieve it every afternoon.

The Shoe Shop of my Dreams

Corns and calluses, walk right in,
Bunions met with a beaming grin,
Fallen arches, hammer toes,
We specialise in all of those.

Duck-like walks and massive feet,
Welcomed in from the dusty street,
Swollen ankles, boiling trotters,
All hosed down and clad in Hotters.

Feet that face in two directions,
Feet requiring disinfection,
Kindly shod by smiling teams,
In the shoe shop of my dreams.

Ode to a Jack Russell

Oh WHY must you bark at the postman?
Why must you batter my ears?
I know it seems rum
But the postman has come
Every morning for TWENTY-FIVE YEARS.

The Hat from Hell

Oh my God! It's the hat from Hell,
Oh she made it herself, surely, couldn't you tell?
It looks so preposterous, oh it's absurd!
And what's that on top? It's a ruddy great bird!

Oh no! It's a parrot, oh well, you could cringe!
And what's that she's got drooping over her fringe?
You don't think it likely … you don't wonder whether …
Oh yes! Yes it is, it's a ruddy great feather!

I just can't believe that she's wearing it here!
And what on God's earth is *that* over her ear?
Over her ear Duncan! Under the parrot!
What! If it isn't a ruddy great carrot!

A ruddy great carrot all crusted with soil!
She looks so ridiculous! Like a gargoyle!
With everyone here in respectable tweed!
Wait, what's on the back? Oh, a ruddy great swede!

Oh the shame! Oh the shame! I'd be dropping
   down dead,
It's like a wheelbarrow tipped over her head,
Oh! What a spectacle! Oh, what a fright!
The committee will never get over the slight.

Oh, she's walking towards us! Well, paste on a *smile*,
Dorothy dear! We're admiring your style!
What an ensemble! And oh, what a hat!
Where were you clever enough to find that?

WHAAAT?

Well I *loved* it as soon as I saw the design!
I'm ever so jealous! I wish it were mine,
I could see it was funny and witty and racy,
As soon as you said it was by Philip Treacy.

*T*here was an outcry in the Suffolk town of Aldeburgh when in 2009, harsh penalties were introduced for feeding gulls. The hungry birds were perceived to be such a threat to public health and safety that a person tossing a chip, say, or the malodorous wreckage of a beefburger became liable to a maximum fine of £2,500. I felt this to be unduly hard-hearted. £2,500 is a vast amount of money especially as, when it comes to feeding the seagulls, you don't always have a choice ...

The Seagull

The seagull sits, like all his breed,
Pink of leg and bony-kneed,
Yellow eye prospecting hard,
For any tourist off his guard.

Down below, a pleasant scene,
A family, by the sea washed clean,
With fish and chips upon their laps,
Dad stands to take some family snaps.

Before his lens a creature flies!
Father can't believe his eyes,
Enraged, he bellows 'Oh my God!
A seagull's had me battered cod!'

A vile curse pollutes his lips,
'The b*****d's had me fish and chips!'
On high the bird, triumphant, sleek,
Smacks his vinegary beak.

Watching the Boat Race

What a boat race! What a crew!
It made me find my old canoe,
And, every sinew going 'crack!'
Row up the old duck pond and back.

*S*ome friends lived in a small cottage. One day they went out and bought themselves a new bed, but on delivery day were aghast to find the mattress was too large and cumbersome to pass up their narrow staircase. After removing various banisters and the door frame, it was still impossible to wrestle the mattress upstairs and onto the bed. Finally, in desperation, they took down part of the cottage wall.

Everyone I spoke to about this seemed to have had a mattress drama of their own. One friend said, when she married and moved out of the parental home, she and her father carried a mattress down the main road to her new house. It was a terrific struggle, with both parties fighting to maintain a grip and hold the edges level as a strong wind blew. At one point the mattress rose up in the gale and landed flat across the catseyes in the middle of the busy road. They danced round it in panic, trying desperately to lift it up and continue their halting journey. Only when they reached the house did they notice the four neat handles stitched along the sides for ease of carriage ...

The Mattress up the Stairs

We had our bedroom painted, it was rather tired and dated,
And the curtains had grown shabby where the wasps
   had hibernated,
There were cracks across the ceiling if you gazed around
   on high,
And I loved the carpet once. Although I can't imagine why.

When we had decorated, as it often is the case,
The other items in the room looked dingy, out of place,
The mattress in particular had seen a better day,
A picture of exhaustion, it was shattered, it was grey.

If I'd had a microscope, on looking through the lens,
I knew I'd just see undesirables: dust mites and allergens,
And so as ours was old, and with regard to all these points,
We went to buy a new one to relieve our aching joints.

Well the mattress man bored on about the way that they
  were made,
The pockets and the springing and the buttons and
  the braid,
He had beds made of leather, he had them made of wood,
On and *on* he droned, we thought we'd drop off where
  we stood.

He told us it was *crucial* that our spines were lying straight,
Unlike on our old bed where we scribe a figure eight,
And so we bought a new one, taking note of all his tips,
And looked forward to support at ankles-shoulders-
  knees-and-hips.

We looked fondly at the mattress as it came in from
   the street,
Well, it was something for ourselves, a luxury, a little treat,
We looked forward to the time when we'd be locking up
   the door,
Taking our glucosamine and giving it what for.

On the day it was delivered I was happy as a queen,
It was wrapped magnificently, swathed in polythene,
We carried out the old one and we leant it on the gate,
Intending to fly-tip it at a later, darker date.

We hurried back inside, and we were gaily unawares,
That the new one had a problem; it would not go up
   the stairs!
It would not go up the stairs! It was too rigid, wide
   and strong,
We angled it and dangled it but no, we'd got it wrong.

My man took up the challenge with defiance on his face,
He took away the banister encroaching on the space,
The door came off its hinges, the frame came off and split,
He sweated and he fretted and it didn't help a bit.

We tried it soft and gentle, we tried it mean and rough,
We got it up a little way, but nothing like enough,
He heaved it with his shoulder, I was hauling from above,
But the mattress wasn't shifting, not for money,
   not for love.

Well, I kicked it in the label and I kicked it in the springs,
I kicked it in the piping and the little button things,
You could tell that it despised us as it flopped this
   way and that,
It said 'I hope you break your ankle, kick away
   you daft old bat!'

Then *laugh*, we had convulsions, we were helpless,
   couldn't stop,
We laughed up to the moment when he felt his back
   go 'pop',
Now he is moaning, he is groaning, it's a grim state
   of affairs,
And he'll have to suffer standing ...
                     as we can't get up the stairs.

Dog Pearly Gates

a sketch

∽

Cast: 1st Angel   Felicity
        2nd Angel   Pam
        Benjie   An old mongrel dog

FELICITY and PAM are angels at the Pearly Gates. FELICITY is playing a harp.

(Harp music suitable for the Pearly Gates)

PAM   Shhhhh! Stop playing that harp!

(Harp music stops)

FELICITY   Why? I'm supposed to play it, I'm an angel at the Pearly Gates.

PAM   I know, so am I, but someone's coming. Look, down the path.

FELICITY   Crikey, it's a dog. Are we expecting anybody? Have a look in the ledger.

PAM   Yes, here it is look. Benjie, elderly dog, road traffic accident, Tottenham Court Road 3 p.m. this afternoon.

FELICITY   Poor animal. He looks all in. *(Calls)* Come on Benjie, not much further!

PAM   Well done Benjie! Now you can have a nice sit down!

BENJIE   Oh, I'm absolutely finished. What a long path! Where IS this place? What happened?

FELICITY   *(Lightly)* What do you think happened, Benjie?

BENJIE   Well I don't know, I found this ball. In the park. I was on my own, as usual, and I was just nosing it along. I suddenly realised I was on the road and then I looked up and saw a bus! A bendy bus. I thought I was a gonner!

COR! Look at those GATES! They're so white and shiny, somebody important must live here!

PAM   Yes.

BENJIE   But is it a good *home*? I've had enough of rubbish homes, tied up all day, just in everybody's way.

FELICITY   Was your last home like that?

BENJIE   After my master died it was. Real rubbish. I'd had such a nice master. I miss him every day. He used to wear a tweed hat you know, and he carried a stick. He used to do this special whistle just for me. They told me he'd died but I still looked for him. I searched for him every day, but I never found him.

        … So is this a good home, would you say?

PAM   This is a *really* good home Benjie. You look through these gates. See all those fields and hedges? The nice wood and that lake for swimming?

BENJIE   Oh I love a dip. I could never get one down the Tottenham Court Road.

FELICITY   Well you can have as many as you like here.

BENJIE   And can I go and sniff *anywhere*?

PAM   Anywhere you fancy. On your own or with the other dogs. Now, you're tired, let's get you settled in. See those kennels on the left-hand side?

BENJIE   Yes, very plush …

FELICITY   Yours is the third one on the left, with the blue
           drinking bowl outside. There's a lovely clean
           bed and a bowl of your favourite, let me look
           in the ledger ... Beefy Treats, is that right?

BENJIE   How did you know THAT? The third kennel
          on the left you say ...

          (*Pause*)

          Who's that bloke standing by my kennel then?

PAM   What bloke is that?

BENJIE   (*Embarrassed*) Oh, stupid, for a minute there
          I thought ... I thought it might have been
          my master ... it's somebody wearing a tweed
          hat ...

FELICITY   A tweed hat?

BENJIE   And ... carrying a stick.

PAM   Perhaps you ought to go and investigate,
          Benjie ...

BENJIE   He's doing my special whistle! I believe it IS
          my master! I think I must have died and gone
          to Heaven!

(*Sound of scampering feet as he tears off*)

FELICITY   *(Quietly)* Funny you should say that Benjie ...

PAM   *(Quietly)* Could be *exactly* what you've done.

Halloween

I ate a lethal mushroom,
I served it up on toast,
That tapping on your shoulder ...
It's me ... I'm a ghost.

Jubilee

Dad took me to our local pub in 1953,
They had a television set, the first I'd ever see,
To watch a Coronation! I knew it sounded grand,
Although at six years old, the word was hard to understand.

But little kids like me, and others all around the world,
We saw the magic crown; we saw magnificence unfurled,
A brand new Queen created, the emergence and
    the birth,
And the Abbey seemed a place between the Heavens
    and the Earth.

Certain pictures linger when considering the reign,
Hauntingly in black and white, a platform and a train,
The saddest thing I ever saw, more sharp than
    any other,
Prince Charles, the little boy who had to shake hands
    with his mother.

I will stand up and be counted; I am for the monarchy,
And if they make mistakes, well they are frail like you
    and me.
I would not choose a president to posture and to preen,
Live in a republic? I would rather have the Queen.

A thousand boats are sailing, little ships among the large,
Close beside the splendour that bedecks the Royal Barge,
And as the pageant passes, I can see an image clear,
Of the Royal Yacht *Britannia*; she should surely have
    been here.

I wish our Queen a genuinely joyful Jubilee,
Secure in the affection of the mute majority,
I hope she hears our voices as we thank her now as one,
Sixty years a Queen. A job immaculately done.

How We Laughed when
Father went Deaf

How we laughed when our father went deaf,
We thought him as daft as a brush,
But now, as we shout 'WHAT?' and 'PARDON?'
I hope he is laughing at us.

Did I Turn Off my Tongs?

We are off for a treat, it's my birthday today,
To London. We're seeing a musical play!
Though I love all the dancing and know all the songs,
All I can think is: 'Did I turn off my tongs?'

Did I turn off the tongs? Well I just cannot say,
My ghastliest fears are rampaging away,
I fret, while pretending to savour the drive,
Are flames licking round my Chanel N°5?

And mentally, throughout the show and applause,
I check our insurance to look for the clause,
That says any payout is shrouded in doubt,
If you don't turn your tongs off before you go out.

Is my beautiful bathroom now swirling in smoke?
Is my orchid bent over and starting to choke?
They will burn through the worktop and into the drawer,
If they haven't already set fire to the floor.

I can *smell* it, can smell the most acrid of pongs,
As my carpet dissolves under hot curling tongs,
I can *hear* it, the hiss and the roar and the crackle,
An inferno out of my hairdressing tackle.

Oh, *please*, as I twiddled the hair round my face,
When every last twiddle was twiddled in place,
Did I put the equipment back where it belongs?
Did I flick off the switch? *Did I turn off the tongs?*

I'm seeing the ruins, all smoking and black,
The fire brigade hoses now useless and slack,
The shock on the face of the horrified throngs,
At the fate of those failing to turn off their tongs.

Much later we sit in the restaurant dim,
He's smiling at me and I'm smiling at him,
On this night which has hit him so hard in the pocket,
I think: 'Did I pull the plug out of the socket?'

And when we get home and we sigh and we stop,
And the day out has been a phenomenal flop,
I hurry upstairs where I splutter and scoff,
The birthday was ruined. The tongs were turned off.

*S*earching through my muddled wardrobe one day, I was ashamed to find that I had packed so many clothes onto the rail that it was impossible to force my fingers between the hangers.

Suffused with guilt, I imagined a time when the wardrobe was stuffed so intolerably full that finally, in the dead of night, it exploded ...

The Exploding Wardrobe

Last night our wardrobe split its seams,
We lay, transported by our dreams,
When through the velvet of the night,
The woodwork cracked! We sat up, white,
We heard it blow; our blood ran cold,
The dovetail joints they could not hold,
The darkness churned, our bedroom shook,
As terrified, we turned to look,
And through the chaos and debris,
We saw the shot mahogany.

Stuffed beyond endurance now,
The thing had split from stern to bow,
The back exploded! Hit the wall,
The sides were splinters, that was all,
Too weak to hold another frock,
The rail collapsed from metal shock,
And clothes too tightly crammed to use,
Dropped upon the heap of shoes,
While loosened from the shattered door,
The lock had rolled across the floor.

Now, as I go upon my way,
That wardrobe on my conscience lay,
Its friendly presence might still loom,
In the corner of our room,
Had I not, for years untold,
Purchased clothes for hot, for cold,
The woollies warm, the cotton cool,
For weddings, holidays and Yule,
Hoping winter, summer, spring,
To one day find, that perfect thing.

Sometimes I'm big, sometimes I'm small,
But I've got clothes to fit them all,
Adding to them day by day,
I never give a thing away,
Embroideries and lace and leather,
And nothing ever goes together.
Too filled with clothes, my wardrobe burst,
Now in my grief I fear the worst,
For in my purse I'll have to dig,
To buy another twice as big.

The Wrong Thing

I like to wear The Wrong Thing
It gives the guests a smile,
I've always gone with The Wrong Thing on,
And stuck out half a mile.

I am thinking of starting a campaign to increase the age of women selling make-up in department stores. Being now of a certain age, I find that a profusion of lines, dark shadows and age spots have come to besmirch my once-radiant visage.

I would like to seek the advice of a supportive make-up lady in her perfumed department-store domain, and after a friendly exchange leave the premises laden with pots of miracle-working lotions sure to reverse the decline.

Unfortunately, this never happens. Instead, I enter the fancy store looking shifty and feeling ill at ease amid the urban smartness. I look doubtfully at the make-up counters and the salesgirls in particular. They all look about fourteen, and are of such exquisitely perfect appearance that I feel like Stonehenge.

Dispirited, I turn my lived-in face to the door and slink away.

The Make-up Lady

I went to buy a lipstick, and I hoped for some advice,
On choosing an attractive shade, to make my face
   look nice,
I stepped up to the counter in my trainers and my mack,
But the sales assistant saw me and she vanished
   out the back.

She was absolutely flawless and an advertiser's dream,
She was icy as a glacier and chic in the extreme,
I was clearly not the customer that she desired to meet,
I could have been some reptile that had crawled in
    off the street.

And I thought I'd find the manager and have a little word,
In favour of an altogether craggier old bird,
Some game old gal who's been around the block
    a time or three,
Who is fending off the years and has a waist as
    thick as me.

An understanding confidante with whom you could relax,
Who *knows* the way that lipstick tends to bleed into
    the cracks,
A saviour for those of us who know our youth is past,
To show us all the tricks and keep us fighting
    to the last.

Had a Little Work Done

O Botox, O Botox, I'm ever so keen,
To look as I looked at the age of sixteen,
Induce paralysis, do as I ask,
Give me, O give me a face like a mask.

O take up a surgical bicycle pump,
And give me some lips that are lovely and plump,
Young men will stagger and say 'Oh my God!
Here comes Pam Ayres … and she looks like a cod!'

Bling

It's never been my thing,
Bling.
For preference of course,
A horse.

The Racehorse Fred

This is the final will and testament,
Of me, of Fred the horse,
For I am running in the National,
And I may not stay the course,
So of my wishes and intentions,
This will be the legal proof,
From me, the racehorse Fred,
Me being sound in mind and hoof.

Now I have not much to leave,
But, anxious to avoid the fate,
Should I fall at Becher's Brook,
Of therefore dying intestate,
I bequeath to my friend Bob,
The haynet where I daily chomped,
And my rug, but he's a Shetland,
So he may be rather swamped.

Bob and I have stood together,
In the sunshine and the rain,
He will be the one to miss me,
If I don't come home again.
To my dear stable companion,
Who will be down in the dumps,
I leave my pack of Polos,
And my bag of sugar lumps.

For I was bred to race,
A thoroughbred is what I am,
From the time I was a foal,
Safe in the paddock with my dam,
My mother, such a mare,
Her velvet muzzle and her scent,
And our stallion was a champion,
But I never met the gent.

I see my jockey now,
I see with grins his face is plastered,
I see him flex his whip,
The little spiteful short-arsed b*****d,
For him, my lucky horseshoe,
He might like to bear in mind,
That I kicked it off at Chepstow,
And it hit the bloke behind.

I don't think people care,
About the *horse* that they have backed,
At twenty-five to one,
At Kempton Park or Pontefract,
It's the fortune won or squandered,
It's the shiver down the spine,
It's the flutter of the racing silks,
Across the finish line.

Now I canter to the start,
Imagining the final scene,
I may be greeted as a hero,
Or be down, behind a screen.
We are under starter's orders,
Blood and labourer and toff
All are roaring in our ears,
It's death or glory boys …
We're off.

The Leather Trousers

a sketch

⌒

FELICITY and PAM are middle-aged old friends. Their families have left home and they now live next door to one another with their respective husbands.

(Knock on door. Footsteps crossing hall)

(PAM opens door to FELICITY)

PAM Hello Felicity, what's up?

FELICITY Oh hi Pam, this Neighbourhood Watch meeting, can we have it at your house? My Roger is half dead with a cold.

PAM 'Course we can. What time? Who's coming?

FELICITY Two-thirty. About fifteen people from our road and Constable Stevens who's giving the talk.

PAM It'll be fine, I'll have a quick tidy up. Will they want tea and bisc …

(Roar of mighty engine)

FELICITY Oh my God Pam, what's that?

PAM You may well ask. It's Gordon with his retirement present to himself. He's just collected it. It's the car of his dreams.

(Car door slams. Gordon's footsteps crunching on gravel coming towards us)

PAM You got it then Gordon! Good grief! What on *earth* are you doing in that get up?

GORDON *(He is absolutely besotted with the car)* This *get up*? You don't think I'm going to drive a car like *that* in my old tweeds do you? I've waited all my working life for this Aston Martin and by God, I'm going to look the part.

PAM I know Gordon, but black leather trousers …

GORDON What's the matter with them?

PAM Well, aren't they a bit … tight? Turn round. They remind me of something in our old grocer's shop. A cheese wire.

FELICITY Yes, they make me think of my Uncle Alec. He had a strangulated hernia. Tight trousers like that aren't good for a man you know Gordon. They can affect the … appendage.

GORDON   Ah, you two, you're just a pair of old fuddy-duddies. You look at me and think I've merely retired, but my situation is far beyond that. I'm free, *free* at last. My spirit is going to soar. Top down, wind in my hair …

PAM   Well there's plenty of it. You've let it get all long and straggly.

GORDON   You can mock! I'll turn the women's heads!

FELICITY   Turn their what?

PAM   And what's that thing on your head?

GORDON   Ah yes, this vintage leather motorist's helmet with intrinsic goggle. From the roaring twenties! The lenses have yellowed a bit but the last thing they saw was Brooklands. And Fangio!

PAM   I don't know what you're on about. You look like Biggles. Let's have a look at this car then.

FELICITY   I've never much cared for bottle green.

GORDON   *(Through gritted teeth)* It's *British Racing Green.*

(Feet crunch on gravel as they walk round car)

    No fingering it, you two. No sitting on the bonnet.

PAM   Strewth! It's enormous. It's squashed my hebe.

FELICITY It's like a tank!

PAM   It'll never go in the garage.

FELICITY What does it do to the gallon?

GORDON   Er. What?

PAM   You heard. What does it do to the gallon?

GORDON   Er, on a long run. Eight.

PAM   Eight miles to the gallon? It's going to
           bankrupt us!

GORDON   Oh LISTEN to you and your petty little
           penny-pinching remarks! Just *look* at it! It's a
           work of art. Just feel it, feel the depth of the
           paintwork ... oh darling ...

PAM   You never stroke me like that.

GORDON   You don't do sixty miles an hour from a
           standing start.

FELICITY   Get in then. Let's see you in it.

(FX Car door opening. Sound of ripping leather)

GORDON   Oh stone the crows! My leather trousers! The
           crotch has gone! What am I going to do?

PAM   Eek! The appendage!

FELICITY   Well I don't know, but in view of the fact that
           fifteen women and Constable Stevens from
           Neighbourhood Watch are coming up the
           drive ...

PAM   How about sixty miles an hour from a standing
           start?

The Wildlife Garden

The wildlife in our garden,
It fills me with delight,
The sparrowhawk attacks by day,
The muntjac comes by night,
The fox is round the dustbins,
The rats they are not pretty,
The squirrel's on the peanuts
And I'm moving to the city.

The Old Twilight Home

At the Old Twilight Home we are safely installed,
Helpless, incontinent, toothless and bald,
Silent but for the occasional shout,
When carers come in here and knock us about.

Our daughters and sons they have fled to a man,
They throw off their parents as fast as they can,
They sometimes drive past looking wealthy and flash,
Having sold off the mansion and trousered the cash.

We just don't deserve to be left in this fix!
Our kids never boarded until they were six!
Discarded, disgruntled, dismayed by our plight,
If this is the twilight then bring on the night.

A few years ago we decided to plant a hedge. We have a small herd of cattle and thought that two smaller fields would be more useful than one big one. A hedge would be an attractive way to divide it, and unlike a barbed wire fence it would change with the seasons and provide homes for small creatures.

I had no idea what a lovely project this would be, how you could sit with a catalogue of hedging plants and put together your own special mixture, like a recipe for a cake. It felt very self-indulgent. I chose holly for Christmas, hawthorn for creamy flowers and bird food, dog-roses for their delicate fragrance and hips, honeysuckle for the beautiful late-night perfume, spindle for its shapely berries in such a ludicrous shade of pink, sloes for making sloe gin and so on. All the little slips were planted like flimsy unpromising sticks and the whole thing was fenced in to deter rabbits.

Over the years, it thickened up. Unabashed by its wispy appearance, it shot skywards, all the various plants enmeshing and knitting together. From year one it was a delight. After its first proper cut this winter, it looks like the *real thing. Still short in stature of course, but undeniably a proper hedge. Birds flit along its length, build their nests and sing with gusto. I walk beside it with my dogs on most days of the year and there is always something interesting to see.*

We have two dogs of our own, and I often look after two more belonging to our son and daughter-in-law. One is a beautiful black Labrador called Crumpet. At this time something had frightened her; she was nervous and lacking in confidence. This was evidenced on walks by her wanting to keep me in sight at all times. One day we were sauntering along and somehow Crumpet had finished up on the wrong side of the new hedge; this didn't matter because, as it was short, she could still see me over the top. Our other dog, a crabby but much-loved Jack Russell named Tats, was lame with a sore paw. The dew claw had snapped near the base, painfully exposing the quick. She was not enjoying the walk and limped along grim-faced, saying 'Me foot! Me foot! How much further?' She seemed worse than when we started out, so I made the mistake of kneeling down to inspect the poorly paw. Crumpet, on the other side of the hedge, suddenly couldn't see me. Gripped by anxiety, she took a short run, leapt up and sailed over the top.

Standing up from looking at the foot, I was struck an enormous smothering blow by the unusual projectile of a hefty black Labrador. There was a thudding impact and I was knocked flat. Lying in the field, the sky and trees revolved around me in comic-book fashion. It was some time before I could stand up and stagger home.

That afternoon I was going to a silver band concert, and especially looking forward to it because my niece, who plays the flugelhorn with great fluidity and beauty, was taking part. Once seated in the auditorium, however, I developed a powerful headache no flugelhorn could ease. It was dire; it throbbed like a drum. I realised this was the sort of scenario where any sensible person would go to a doctor, and I imagined the conversation I might have with him when I got there. 'Tell me Mrs. Russell,' he would say, 'how did you sustain the head injury?' and I would reply, 'Oh, I was hit by a flying crumpet.'

Crumpet is also afraid of the toaster. This sounds hilarious but is in fact desperately sad to see. During the last tense, clicking moments before toast erupts from the fiery depths, the dog quakes pitifully beneath the table.

I wrote this for her as a consolation ...

The Terrifying Toaster

Our Labrador is nervous of the toaster,
When we use it she is paralysed with fright,
And it doesn't make the slightest bit of difference,
Whether we use wholemeal, granary or white,
We used to hope she'd scare away intruders,
And bark at burglars, that would have been nice,
But no, *we* have to put our arms around *her*,
And say 'Don't worry, only one more slice!'

Two Little Crumpets

I've found a private swimming pool,
It's called a cattle trough,
But every time I take a dip,
I seem to get told off!

I like to snap at wasps,
I find it quite diverting,
But this one's rather hot,
And now my face is hurting …

A September Song

He is off to university, all is now in place,
There is fear, anticipation and excitement in his face,
An overstuffed enormous bag and rucksack in the hall,
And a ghastly leaden feeling like the ending
   of it all.

I cannot let it show, this selfish aching in my heart,
For the sweet chaotic years in which you played the
   major part,
I am fearful of the emptiness when you depart the room,
And silence settles round us like the stillness
   of a tomb.

At your bedroom door I used to stand and shake my head,
The mess was unbelievable, the floor, the chair, the bed,
The place was never hoovered, never felt a duster's touch
But now it's neat and clean and I don't like it
   half as much.

I loved you going out, so young and eager and alive,
I loved you coming home, your little car turned in the drive,
The energy, the racket, all the songs you like to play,
And I won't know where to turn to
    when the music dies away.

There was ringing of the mobile, there was tapping of
    the text,
The iPod and the iPad and the new thing coming next,
There was passion, there was fashion, with your father
    in despair
Saying 'IN the name of GOD what has that BOY
    done to his HAIR?'

Now parents realise that all between them which
    has dwindled,
Can be resuscitated and romantically rekindled,
Old passions reignited, sexual energies uncurbed,
But looking at your Dad, I think I'll leave them
    undisturbed.

My son is ready, independent, eager, fit, he *has* to go,
He must take his chances now!
    I know, I know, I know, I *know!*
He will make so many friends, he will be having such
    a ball,
It may all be so exciting … that he won't come home
    at all.

I'm looking at a life which seems so drained of all its colour,
The heart is gone from us; we are older, we are duller,
Now if people ask us, we'll show photographs and say,
'He's up at university. That's right. He lives away.'

*T*he first time I observed preparations for a modern wedding at close quarters was when our eldest son married in 2010. Prior to that, I had seen my brothers and sister marry in various village churches in the 1960s. Things have changed. The modern wedding is as beautiful and significant as ever, but new elements have appeared in the intervening decades. Now there is a ravishing choice of venue both at home and abroad: castles, hotels, forests, the white shores of the Caribbean. In addition to the bridegroom's traditional stag night, the modern bride-to-be now has a hen night. Along with her friends she might luxuriate in some perfumed spa, paint pottery for a souvenir dinner service or fly away to the sun. The giving of wedding presents is no longer random. The young couple identify their choices and set up a department store list, so that there is no guesswork. Guests see exactly what is desired, and they buy the items they can afford.

There is a great deal to organise. The wedding finery, marquee and flowers, the booking of the band, the now-expected, professional-looking first dance by the bride and groom, readings, speeches and, crucially, the provision of fine food, a warm environment and lavish, well-chosen wines to complement all. Finally a dramatic departure and honeymoon in some enticing far-off destination. The amount of planning, preparation and outlay required for a perfect day can be colossal.

Now compare this with the weddings of my brothers and sister in the 1960s. These were equally lovely and enjoyable events but much was done in-house. Someone in the village who was 'good with a needle' would make the bridal dress. Someone else, good at cake-making, would make the cake. Weddings always took place in the flower-filled village church and the reception was held in the village hall, bedecked with balloons for the occasion. Along the stage would be arrayed an eclectic selection of wedding gifts. Duplication was a common hazard and I once saw three dustbins all given by different well-wishers. One frequently offered gift was a set of three lidded Pyrex dishes.

The Co-op was popular for catering and did a good ham tea for eight shillings a head. After the cake was cut, the bride discreetly slipped away to reappear in her going-away suit. In the meantime several baked-bean tins had been tied to the back of their car. Soon the young couple were ready to leave and filed outside followed by all the guests. They would be waved off to a chorus of clattering tin cans and hysterical beer-fuelled laughter, whereupon everybody picked up their belongings and went home.

By six o'clock, it was all over.

Don't Ask Me to the Wedding

∽

So your daughter's getting married! And your fine
    athletic son,
Send my love and warm congratulations to them,
    every one,
I wish them health and happiness and joyful
    expectation,
But don't ask me to the wedding. Do not send
    the invitation.

It's not that I don't care, or am too mean to send
    a gift,
I just know that at the wedding, every grievance,
    every rift,
Every bitter family feud that simmered slowly
    down the years
Will come boiling to the surface after one
    too many beers.

I do not have to be there! I can still describe the day,
The best man he'll be nervous, the vicar he'll be gay,
The ushers will be pimply, the babies will all shriek,
And ex-wives and ex-husbands look with loathing
    and don't speak.

Oh the fragrance of the flowers, the stained glass
    like a jewel,
The murmur of the organ and the bridesmaids
    minuscule,
The shyness of the couple, their tenderness and tears,
You'd never guess they'd lived together now
    for seven years.

The couple cut the cake, and on the knife each
    placed a hand,
The best man made a speech but he was drunk
    and couldn't stand,
We clapped for all the speakers and our duty did
    not shirk,
Although we couldn't hear, the microphone,
    it didn't work.

We're ready for the sausage rolls, we're ready for
    the ale,
We're ready for the feast, no point in letting it
    get stale,
I'm piling up my plate and then I'm going back for
    more,
To fortify myself before I get out on that floor!

Three things to fill your heart with dread and make
    your innards shrivel:
A marquee and a disco and a DJ spouting drivel,
He's pumping up the volume, cranking up the
    flashing lights,
And there's women dancing barefoot
    with their feet stuck through their tights.

Old bones and hip replacements, they are grinding
    off the dust,
Grandpa's doing a kind of geriatric pelvic thrust,
'The Shake', 'The Locomotion', the Conga and 'The
    Twist',
And the whole pulsating bunch are getting
    absolutely … intoxicated.

Gyrating, undulating, it is sweaty and it's hot,
Separate and desperate, we're dancing on the spot,
An elbow in the back; a sharp stiletto in the shin,
And there's lechery, treachery, darkly in the din.

It's not polite to leave before the couple, it is said,
But still a vision rises of a warm and comfy bed,
A nice electric blanket and a pillow soft and deep,
The party rages on. I wish I was at home asleep.

So don't ask me to the wedding, I insist, it's for the
    best.
Send my invitation to some bright and youthful guest,
And for now let's toast the couple; let true love take
    its course
And in a couple of years I'll come and drink
    to the divorce.

*R*umour has it that I was once employed as a spy, but of course you wouldn't expect me to comment ...

MI6

In my cloak and dagger I,
Made my living as a spy,
In creepy, dark, suspenseful scenes,
I blew their trains to smithereens.

Allotment Rustler

I like to see allotments for the architecture's grand,
The sheds and huts, the water butts, the sweetness of
   the land.
But no! As night is falling, the shamelessness!
   The folly!
Some lowlife has flashed a knife, and made off with
   your cauli!

That darned allotment rustler, he has come to do us wrong!
We'll lash him with a leaky hose! We'll prick him with
   a prong!
He'll never prowl these parts again, or steal another cauli,
Then round our plants we'll do a dance and crack a bottle
   o' Bolly!

Boyfriend to Stay

a sketch

❧

PAM and GORDON are a middle-aged couple. It is Friday afternoon and they are in their sitting room discussing the arrival of their daughter Katie …

PAM   Just think Gordon, our little daughter bringing her boyfriend home for the weekend!

GORDON   *(Not at all happy)* Mmm. When's he coming?

PAM   Tonight, they're getting here about seven o'clock.

GORDON   *(Ratty)* What's he do, this bloke anyway?

PAM   Sholto. His name's Sholto. He works in the media.

GORDON   *(Sarcastic)* Oh, and where's that?

PAM   What's got into you Gordon? I think you're jealous. I know she's always been 'your little girl' but now she's got herself a boyfriend and you don't like it. Your nose has been put out of joint.

GORDON Oh don't talk such unremitting rubbish … Where's he going to sleep, this Sholto?

PAM Well with Katie, I imagine.

GORDON **_WHAT?_**

PAM Well, surely you don't imagine they're not sleeping together already?

GORDON My little Katie!

PAM She's twenty-three Gordon.

GORDON Well I'm not having it.

PAM You're not, no.

GORDON No, it's my house and I'm not having it. That bed is right above the kitchen. And it's always squeaked. I'm not sitting there eating my All-Bran in the morning, listening to my daughter and some opportunist directly overhead!

PAM What do you mean, some opportunist? She's probably going to MARRY him!

GORDON Well, that's different. That's sanctified bonking. I wouldn't *mind* that so much. It's sort of a chore, like getting the coal in.

PAM   Thanks. That explains a lot.

GORDON *(Voice dripping scorn)* Sholto indeed!

PAM   His father's a banker.

GORDON A what?

PAM   A banker.

GORDON Got a few bob has he? No doubt from sucking the blood of his fellow man.

PAM   They live in that beautiful white house on the Davenport Road.

GORDON *(More interested)* What, that house with the Range Rovers outside? And the Humvee?

PAM That's the one.

GORDON That place with the enormous conservatory and tennis court?

PAM Yes.

GORDON With the post and rail paddocks and the stud?

PAM Mmm, that's the place.

GORDON Got any 3-in-1?

PAM Why?

GORDON I'm going up to fix the squeak.

If You Gave Me a Diamond

∽

If you gave me a diamond as big as a rock,
Apart from the fact I would pass out from shock,
I'd fear I would lose it, or burglars would reap it,
So all things considered, I think you should keep it.

The Swifts

The swifts are back!
They slice the air,
They're back! They're back!
From God knows where,
Navigating, mile on mile,
To the very roof,
To the very tile.

Tippy Tappy Feet

The days are slowly passing since I found her still
 and prone,
Since I took her to the surgery and came back on my own,
Now, as my key turns in the lock, the sound I miss
 the most of all,
Are the tippy tappy toenails as they skidded
 down the hall.

There was something in the welcome; there was
 something in her style,
In the jingle of her collar and ecstatic doggy smile,
The tail that wagged so furious, the eyes that shone
 so bright,
It's the silence. It's the silence. It is blacker than the night.

And if I'd had a rotten day, if I was tired and spent,
If I had found indifference in every place I went,
Always at my journey's end, when I was flat and lonely,
That little dog convinced me I was someone's
 one and only.

Her things are still around me, I have left them all alone,
A little greasy collar, a yellow rubber bone,
A hairy tartan blanket in her basket on the floor,
From which she sprang to terrify all knockers at the door.

How grievous is the emptiness on entering the hall,
How disproportionate; so great a loss for one so small,
For the music it is missing, and my home is incomplete,
The music of her tippy tappy doggy dancing feet.

*M*y niece received the gift of a friendship cake 'starter', which is usually a jam jar filled with yeasty dough, a kind of edible chain letter. It comes with instructions on adding flour, sugar, etc., with the idea of eventually baking it as a cake. Peculiarly, these things have names, in this case Herman the German. For ten days or more, the mixture sits in a warm kitchen waiting for its next snack. When large and bloated, the dough is divided into four, three parts are given to friends and the fourth part baked as a cake. Having eaten the result, my niece and her family were ill for weeks. The one person in the family who didn't feel peckish at the time and refused a slice was perfectly well.

A Friendship Cake

A man gave me a friendship cake,
I'd never met the fella,
We served it up for Sunday tea,
And all got salmonella.

I wrote this for Freshfields Donkey Village near Buxton in Derbyshire, a charity which rescues ill-treated and vulnerable donkeys. Children with special needs come to stay and as part of their visit, help to look after the animals. Both donkeys and children seem to appreciate the arrangement very much.

Dreaming of Fresh Fields

I would like to think there is a place for me,
With clean water to drink, and a shady tree,
Where someone cared if I had enough to eat,
And brushed my coat, and trimmed my feet.

I would like to be with other donkeys too,
With boys and girls to hug me, and love me true,
I would like to be with people who are kind,
Where, when I die, someone will notice,
     Someone will mind.

Count Me Out

Once I knew everybody who lived down this street,
Now I daren't make eye contact with people I meet.
I keep my head down and I look at my feet
When I'm out.

I did have a pension but not any more,
It went through the roof, then it went through the floor,
I paid on the nail; now I wonder what for.
I got nowt.

That family doctor you loved and adored
Who rushed out at night in a clapped-out old Ford,
He's gone. A & E and no bed on the ward,
Go without.

In hospitals now you risk MRSA
And under your bedstead the cockroaches play,
If you don't clutch your kidneys, they'll have 'em away,
So look out.

I rang the police. 'You must help me!' I said,
'An axeman is aiming an axe at my head!'
'He'll have had a rough childhood, don't hurt him,'
　　they said,
You old trout.

Ah the dew on the bramble, the lark in the morn,
Those cheery old geezers out cutting the corn,
Hunch over computers now, downloading porn
Drinking stout.

I'm afraid in some old people's home on the green,
Uncaring assistants will talk to me mean,
And make me pay fees till I ain't got a bean,
Clean me out.

Euthanasia's coming, it's too late to run,
Hear the last loving words of a daughter or son:
'You've outstayed your welcome now Ma, here's a gun …'
We're off out.

I can't be a patriot, can't fly the flag
People go round with a bomb in a bag
And my enthusiasm is starting to flag,
It's run out.

Count me out dears, for who cares what I think?
All that's familiar has gone in a blink,
As a puzzled old dinosaur here on the brink,
Count me out.

Sleepless

The lot of the insomniac,
Endless hours dull and black,
The husband snoring, ragged tones,
And worries come to gnaw your bones.

All the restless night I thrashed,
Wild thoughts around the brainbox flashed,
I'm wide awake and I could weep,
Tomorrow I'll be half asleep.

Here comes a damp and fragrant dawn,
I greet it with a red-eyed yawn,
Devoid of any vim or zip,
And desperate for a decent kip.

I would spring with joy and vigour,
Cut an energetic figure,
Radiant and fine and sprightly,
Had I slept all through the nightly.

On a Gardeners' World *television programme I was enthusing about certain easy-to-grow plants which not only look nice, but which* also benefit wildlife by providing pollen, nectar and berries. *Pyracantha is one of my favourites.*

The Pyracantha Anthem

On many a flower, shrub and tree,
Food for birds grows naturally,
On the pyracantha say,
As autumn shortens each new day,
See the show of berries start!
In red and green, to lift the heart,
And after we've admired the spot,
Blackbirds come and scoff the lot!

*T*his is about one of those homes monopolised by the family dog. He is a perfectly nice animal if a bit nondescript, but every conversation is either interrupted by him, or revolves about his various not-particularly-fascinating qualities. The dog can do no wrong. His owner, believing you to be as besotted as she is herself, makes a point of never talking about anything else.

Barking

You made it! I so hoped you'd call in on your way to town!
Have you met our new dog Charlie? He's a character,
   GET DOWN!
Yes, he's *very* spotty, you could take him for a leopard!
Breed? I think he's corgi with a touch
   of German Shepherd.

In you come! I'll take your coat, sit down on that settee,
Oh, hold on just a second, I think Charlie needs a wee,
Out you go then Charlie! Do a wee-wee on the grass,
Oh no. It's more substantial. Mind your shoes
   when you go past.

Now, what can I get you? Tea or coffee? Vodka? Gin?
Oh, hold on just a minute, Charlie's barking to come in,
IN YOUR BED NOW CHARLIE!
   Oh, he wants to lick your hand!
He's always eating bird muck, *why*, I cannot understand.

IN YOUR BASKET CHARLIE! Stop that
   scratching! Where's your toy?
I worry over Charlie, he's a lovely little boy,
We got him from the dogs home,
   I don't say he'd been abused,
Charlie! Here! Fetch! Stay! Shake hands!
   You see? He seems confused.

Here's a cappuccino, chocolate sprinkled on the froth,
Biscuit? NOT YOU CHARLIE!
   Oh my God! I'll get a cloth.
It's gone all down your cardigan! It must have soaked
   right through!
Thank God it's just a shabby old worn-out one.
   Oh. It's new.

Oh no! How disappointing! Must you really go so soon?
I hoped you'd stay with me and Charlie all the
   afternoon,
Love to everyone at home … be sure to close the gate …
Be careful of your sandals round the obstacle!
   Too late.

R
egarding a controversial seaside sculpture:

Doom in Ilfracombe

∽

The residents of Ilfracombe,
How they must have sinned,
A seaside first, by Damien Hirst,
A pregnant woman, skinned.

A curse has fell on Ilfracombe,
I see the tourists clear,
From many lands all holding hands,
And jumping off the pier.

All Aboard the Ark *or*
The Bigot's Ballad

❦

All aboard, all aboard, all aboard the Ark,
Find yourselves a cabin quick, the times are getting dark,
I hate to leave my homeland; it cuts me like a knife,
But all aboard the Ark to save the English way of life.

No football hooligans, no yobs, no thugs or mischief makers
No ladyboys from old Bangkok, no mincing poodlefakers,
No deviants, no hoodies, no itinerants, no way,
And no nomadic persons eating hedgehogs baked in clay.

Nobody using chopsticks, talking oriental twaddle,
And nobody obese 'cause I don't want to watch 'em waddle
No one from Newcastle with their Geordie mumbo jumbo,
And nobody from Birmingham, Karachi or Colombo.

No reiki head massagers keen on fingering your scalp,
No acupuncturists with silver pins to make you yelp,
No whingeing hypochondriacs with irritating coughs,
Or rootin', tootin', pheasant-shooting, double-barrelled toffs.

No upper crust aristocrats with footmen and with flunkeys,
No chorizo sausages, no bush meat and no monkeys,
No sushi or sashimi, no kebab or curry lark,
We're having meat and taters. It's a meat and taters Ark.

Only trim athletic people sail along with me,
If you can't sprint up the stairs I'll leave you standing
   on the quay,
No children. No exuberance, no playfulness, no chatter,
And no decrepit fogies with their false teeth all a-clatter.

We're taking up the gangplank and we're casting off the
 ropes,
Setting sail with just our aspirations and our hopes,
Everyone who frightened us has now been swept aside,
All aboard the Ark, we're sailing on the evening tide.

We've a portrait of our noble Queen set high upon the shelf,
So let's all raise a glass … Hold on … *I'm on here by myself!*
The only person on the ship! Our course set for the west,
I excluded *everybody* … this is like *Marie Celeste* …

HELP! Somebody help me! I am stranded all alone!
My little ship is desolate … the wind cuts to the bone …
I'm sailing into stormy seas both treacherous and dark …
All aboard, All aboard, All aboard The Ark.

The Bungled Bid

I bid for a buggy on eBay,
The bidding was frantic and tense,
It's mine and it's nice,
But at four times the price,
I wish I'd had more buggy sense.

Baffled in the Bike Shop

a sketch

∽

PAM   Oh, what a fantastic bike shop! There are hundreds of them all lined up! *(Sniffs)* They smell lovely as well! Sort of oily and rubbery! To think I'm going to have a new bike after all these years! I'll just ask this assistant. Excuse me!

ASST   Yes?

PAM   I wonder if you can help me. I want to buy a new bike.

ASST   Well you're certainly in the right place madam, what kind of thing are you after, conventional shopper with a wicker basket?

PAM   Well no, not really, I was after something a bit sporty.

ASST   Really? I had you down as more of a plodder. Well, we do on- or off-road bikes, Mountain

Bikes, Hybrid, Folding or Lightweight Drop Handlebar. Will you be riding over rocks and boulders?

PAM   Er … No.

ASST   Then can you describe the terrain?

PAM   Terrain? I don't know, I just live in the country, I'm not sure we've got any terrain. I was just going to ride it along the country lanes and down the towpath.

ASST   Yes, but is it an *extreme* towpath?

PAM   I don't think so, no. It's just an ordinary sort of towpath ... with flowers.

ASST   Then I think you need a Hybrid.

PAM   I see. *(She doesn't.)* A hybrid? How high is it?

ASST   No madam. A *Hybrid* is for road, and *light* off-road use, but with Mountain Bike gearing. Have you thought about gearing? What do you think, 27-speed Shimano?

PAM   I haven't got any gears on my old bike. That's why I've got thighs as big as The Ritz.

ASST   And suspension? Will you need full suspension, or just front shocks with hard tails?

PAM   I don't understand what you mean.

ASST   Hard tails. No shocks at the back.

PAM   Well I wouldn't want any shocks at the back.

ASST   Do you know your seat tube length?

PAM   My what?

ASST   Your seat tube length. It provides your standover height, which is the amount of clearance between the top tube or crossbar, and the crotch.

PAM   I've never heard of it.

ASST   The crotch?

PAM   No, the other stuff.

ASST   And then you'll need the clothing madam, it
         doesn't matter what you wear on top, if your
         underclothing does not wick. Wick is my
         watchword, wick wick wick! We have the full
         range of wicking bras, tops and crops … and
         moving on to footwear and helmets …

PAM   No, no, it's all right. Look, don't bother, I'm
         going to pop next door.

ASST   Next door madam? Next *door* is an animal
         sanctuary.

PAM   Yes I know. Getting a bike's too complicated
         for me. I'm going to buy myself a donkey.

The Cycling Holiday

❧

I *went to France recently, on a cycling trip. If I had told my friends I was going on a normal, sun-and-sand kind of holiday, I expect their response would have involved plenty of kind, encouraging advice:*

'You be sure to put your feet up and have a nice rest! You work hard, you deserve it!'

Or they may have visited the very place themselves: 'You'll love it!' they might gush. 'It's so beautiful, I wish we were coming as well!'

The weather would certainly be featured: 'Hope the sun shines! Don't get sunburned!' Concern may be expressed for your wellbeing: 'Safe journey! Let us know when you arrive!' along with saucy notes of the nudge-wink variety: 'Don't do anything I wouldn't do! Mind what you get up to out there!'

These are the kind of remarks you might expect before a normal holiday.

However, if you tell your friends you are going on a cycling holiday, this is not going to be the case. Instead, they smirk, and adopting a strange crab-like walk, sidle up to you and say:

'Well. Mind you don't get a sore arse!'

They then crease up with coarse laughter. Alternatively they may tell you truly execrable cycling jokes of which these two are typical examples:

1. Why couldn't the man make his bicycle stand up?
   Because it was too tyred.
2. My dog chases anybody on a bike!
   What did you do?
   I had to take his bike away.

People were also quick to ask me if I had bought my padded cycling shorts, and I gave this serious thought. The thing was, I had not cycled for years. Decades. A quarter of a century. Yet I was about to set off to France to cycle long distances every day for a week. Not only that, but the friends we were going with were exceedingly fit. One ran regularly in the London Marathon, and all were serious about being in top physical condition. Clearly, I didn't want to be the odd one out, the embarrassing red-faced nuisance puffing at the back, who couldn't keep up, who shouldn't have come. I decided to research what equipment I actually needed, then dispensing with unnecessary affectations, identify and acquire the basics, the absolute essentials.

I found a cycle shop in Cheltenham and set out my case to the disturbingly toad-like man seated in a sunken attitude behind the counter. I was going on a cycling holiday, my companions were fit, experienced cyclists and I wanted to ascertain what equipment I really needed. Take cycling shorts for instance, were they actually essential? What did they do exactly and how were they made? The toad-like man revealed himself to be a pillock. A terrible grin spread over his face:

'You come round 'ere darlin', I'll give yer a guided tour,' he croaked.

I had more luck on the internet. There, I discovered everything I had ever wanted to know about cycling shorts – in particular, that the very best, top-drawer versions are made from chamois leather. This seemed immensely useful to me. If you didn't fancy going for a bike ride, you could take your shorts off and clean all the windows.

We set off. Our starting point was Chinon in the Loire Valley, brooded over by the majestic chateau and awash with fine regional wines. On our first morning we reported to the cycle depot to be furnished with our bikes. Having already supplied our height and leg measurements, only fine-tuning was required – a tweak of the saddle height, a lowering of the handlebar.

Custodian of the depot was Eric, a humourless man who gave two no-nonsense demonstrations. These were a) the repairing of a puncture, and b) how to wrestle your chain back on when it has come off. Eric managed at the same time to infer that anybody who couldn't do either of these *simple tasks should have stayed at home. I watched his deft juggling of the grease-caked chain with misgivings. Finally he gave us his Handy Tips Gleaned After Years of Experience. The first one was particularly startling, delivered as it was in his flat, monotone voice:*

'I recommend a precautionary application of antiseptic cream to the entire crotch area.'

A stunned silence followed. Horrible visions were conjured up.

'So you might, matey,' murmured my husband.

Eric gave us maps of recommended cycling routes and, for our first day, suggested a ride to Château du Rivau. It was stunningly beautiful. Months before, on receiving the various brochures at home, I had cynically leafed through and dismissed the seductive photographs as a mere come-on for tourists.

'There's no way,' I scoffed, 'no way we're likely to see all these beautiful things at once!'

But see them we did. On that day and subsequent days, we pedalled our bikes through fields of sunflowers, their enormous endearing faces all turned in the same direction. Our route took us spinning through vineyards, orchards, melon-fields and forests, all washing like a sea at the base of white castles.

We cruised along the levees of the Loire, wide embankments built to contain the river when in flood. Alongside us, on the verges, householders offered modest

boxes of tomatoes and cucumbers for sale to the cyclists,
and ahead of us shady paths ran away beneath a cool
arching canopy of trees. It was unforgettable. With our
tyres crackling on the sandy surface we rode along, sweet
little homes and gardens on our right, and on our left,
glimpsed through woodland, the sparkle and flash of the
Loire.

I should have written a profound and beautiful poem
about that tranquil and inspiring place. Instead, I wrote this:

Let's go on a cycling holiday!
Let's all be jolly good sports!
With insects all down the back of your throat,
And up the leg of your shorts.

Grinstead

I am Grinstead the puppet horse, I cannot walk or trot,
But from my shoebox stable I'm observing quite a lot,
I see the shapely lady groom arriving with her dog,
The horses all get cuddles and the owner gets a snog.

That Perfect Swimsuit

I'm going on my holidays! I'm going on a cruise!
Earlier I thought this was exhilarating news,
I bought my linen trousers and I bought my stripy top,
But now I need a swimsuit, and my spirits start to drop.

At my lonely fireside I scan the catalogue,
Me, my sinking hopes, a cup of cocoa and the dog,
I see the flawless model as she gazes out to sea,
And *no way* could that outfit ever look the same on me.

That supermodel needs no underwiring or support,
No digital enhancement, she is tall and firm and taut,
Dejectedly I scrutinise the photo in my fist
As I seek the perfect swimsuit, which I
     don't believe exists.

I blame the fashion industry, I blame the magazines,
For only showing swimming suits on young girls in
   their teens,
No roly-poly grannies as they frolic on the shore,
Perfect for the gentleman who likes ... a little more.

I find it hard to grasp the phraseology myself
Would I like a soft-cup, or be better with a shelf?
Should I have a modest leg? Or have it cut to shock,
And when my husband sees me will I be
   a laughing stock?

Do I want the halter neck, the plunging or the scooped?
The fierce elastication to support what might have
   drooped?
I'm throwing down the catalogue, it's all too hard for me,
I'll wear the same old black one that I bought in
   ninety-three.

*O*ur eldest son is now married and I am a mother-in-law. I would like to be considered a good one, because to date our family has given me much joy and interest and I would like this to continue. However, on researching my new position, I felt dejected by the amount of negative comment surrounding the job. It seems that mothers-in-law are automatically assumed to be grim, interfering and critical. The internet teems with corny, old-fashioned jokes. Here is a small but typical selection:

1. A man goes to buy a car. The salesman asks, 'Do you want one with an airbag?' Man replies, 'No thanks, I've got the mother-in-law.'
2. Racehorse trainer to colleague: 'Just look at that horse, what stamina! Stays longer than the mother-in-law.'
3. An anagram of mother-in-law? Woman Hitler.

That mothers-in-law are bad news seems to be a widely held view. In Sydney airport last year I was queuing in one of those concertina-like corridors which extend out to the aircraft door. It was suffocatingly hot and packed with people. I was beside two young women who were discussing a party to be held in Dubai. It was impossible not to overhear their conversation and, again, I found it depressing. The women seemed mercenary and grasping. I heard one say, 'Of course you can't go to the party empty-handed. You've got to take something of some monetary value. But it can be crap.' The other digested this fact for a moment, nodded understandingly and replied, 'Oh. Yeah. Like something your mother-in-law gave you.'

Anxious now, I asked one of my best friends, the mother of a large, all-married family, if she could reveal the secret of being a good mother-in-law. She said nothing, only drew a hand across her mouth to indicate the quick and final closure of a zip.

My Mother was Right About You

There are conquering heroes, it's true,
And decent men, I've known a few,
There are ruthless hard-hitters,
And absolute quitters,
But Mother was right about you.

I hear her voice ringing and pure,
Those warnings I chose to ignore,
She said, 'Look but don't touch,
He won't come to much!'
And Mother knew best, that's for sure.

But what's this you're saying, sweet pea?
That tragically late you can see,
After years of endurance
And paying insurance,
Your mother was right about *me*.

The Paper Ears

Here lies a rabbit, this thick mark on the road,
Pink paper ears blown by the turbulence of
  passing traffic,
Picked by magpies, tugged by crows, shaded by
  buzzards,
A stain, with fragile ears,
Upright.

Yet this was a perfect creature, this rabbit,
This infester of banks, this thief of crops,
Twitcher of nose, liquid dark of eye,
Digger, hop-skip-and-jumper,
Flick of a white scut in the grass.

One rabbit, doe or buck,
Warm fur; glossy from the polished burrow
An adventurer, quick and fecund,
With pink babies deep in the dark earth,
Snug and intertwined.

'Such a pest, such vermin!
Plenty more where that came from!
It's a pity you can't still eat 'em!'
If people spoke their thoughts aloud
This is what the paper ears would hear.

Litter Moron

See the hazel coppices,
Where dainty catkins dance,
Ideal for dumping mattresses,
As soon as I get the chance.

I'll bring me tumble-drier,
And me grandma's three-piece suite,
And tip 'em in the bluebell wood,
With me Honda's old front seat.

I am the litter moron,
I like to spoil the view,
Coming with my rotting junk,
To a beauty spot near you.

The Shakespeare-like Odes

M y books are published by Ebury Press which I have found to be a pleasant, supportive company. The people there are very thoughtful, they send me a card signed by everyone at Christmas, and a bunch of flowers for my birthday.

In common with publishing houses all over the world, Ebury Press are keen for their authors to have a presence on the social networking sites such as Facebook and Twitter. It was suggested to me that by twittering I could gain a whole new demographic. I did not know what that was, but

I knew I wasn't interested. I found all the Twitter jargon off-putting: tweets, retweets, hashtags and handles were not something I wanted to explore. Why would I want to send out little 140-character messages? What would I say? Who would I be saying it to? Oh no, I thought, leave it to young people who enjoy all that sort of thing.

Ebury were not to be easily outflanked, however: they told me they were going to hold a Twitter seminar in their conference room in London. There would be interesting authors, tea and biscuits, and a knowledgeable lady coming to give a talk. It was a chance to find out a little more about it, and to ask any questions. It seemed impolite to refuse, so my husband Dudley and I went along.

A white screen had dropped down from the ceiling and the lecturer stood on the podium. She showed examples of what she considered to be good tweets. They still seemed inane to me, pointless little observations about not much. I asked a few questions in a crabby fashion, and was glad when it ended and we could leave the stuffy room. Outside Dudley and I looked at each other as if to say 'What was all that about!'

Shortly afterwards Ebury rang to say they had established a Twitter account for me. 'You can start tweeting any time you like,' they said. 'It's all set up! Don't hold back! Go for it!' Realising I had been niftily outmanoeuvred, I switched my computer on to have a look.

A little box appeared in which to write my 140-character tweet, a character being a letter, punctuation mark or space. At the time I was trying to write a song called 'Eat More Fruit' and, being immersed in fruity thoughts, composed a little fruity verse:

No fiddlier fruit upon the planet,
Than the rock-hard pomegranate,
See his useful yellow skin,
For keeping all his innards in.

I quite liked this and posted it out to whoever might be on the receiving end. At the time the London 2012 Olympics were just getting into their stride, and with some bemusement I had been watching the female boxing:

See those ladies in the ring,
Gracefully they duck and swing,
Through bloodied teeth they gamely gulp,
And beat each other to a pulp.

I posted this as well. A host of amiable replies came flying back. People said how nice it was to find me on Twitter and I acquired a few followers. I thought I would offer them a little titillation in the form of 'The Erotic Verses':

O come with me if you are able,
It's dead romantic down our stable,
The straw is deep and gold of course,
But first we have to shift the horse.

O take my hand in gesture fond,
It's dead romantic down our pond,
With naked swimming planned for later,
If we dodge the alligator.

O take my hand and dance erratic,
It's dead romantic up our attic,
Side by side we'll shyly blush,
Hearing all the cisterns flush.

O take my hand you fragrant feller,
It's dead romantic down our cellar,
But just before we lose control,
Shovel up that ton of coal.

*I am a Twitter convert now, and tweet Shakespeare-like
odes all the time. Some are tragedies:*

I always have knitted since I was a girl,
I rattle along doing plain, doing purl,
I stitch it together, inspecting each piece,
To just hear, 'No thank you, I'll stick to my fleece.'

Some contain useful fitness advice:

If you've let your body sag,
Pilates ought to be your bag,
Results are great and outlay small,
On your back in the village hall.

Some describe heartbreaking scenes:

I stared at a goosegog for over an hour,
It was small and bewhiskered and rock-hard and sour,
'How unkind!' It said, 'Just how mean can you be?
I fear you are making a fool out of me.'

Some show steely grit and determination:

> I wish I had a swimming pool,
> Beside a patch of shade,
> But Strewth! They cost a bomb,
> So on reflection, pass the spade.

*Some are downright spooky, like this one about the plaintive
cry of a gull:*

> And corpses rolling in the deep,
> Distracted from their restless sleep,
> Through lips of blue pronounce each word:
> 'Won't someone *shoot* that bloody bird.'

Some are exceedingly raunchy:

They were soldiers, they met in the desert,
They were there for the righting of wrongs,
With shuddering chests, they threw off their vests,
And went at it hammer and tongs.

Some give helpful definitions of little-used words:

Pulchritude: Beauty
Just went down the field tonight to see my cows had hay,
Very cold and silent and a fat moon lit my way,
'Here you are my dears!' I cried, 'I've brought you
    extra food!'
But they looked down their noses at my lack of
    pulchritude.

Some are highly political:

'Man shall not live by bread alone'
So sayeth Deuteronomy,
Could be optimistic,
In the light of the economy.

Some are festive:

Christmas comes but once a year,
And fills the populace with fear,
Because they know they somehow must,
Roast taters with a crispy crust.

And some offer profound philosophical advice:

You have to dance while you are able,
Do the can-can on the table,
Grab each chance that flashes past,
For life goes by so deadly fast.

Driving Home

I am driving home. It is two o'clock in the morning.
I see a little house in a lightless village,
Private and closed.

In the house my son sleeps, his young wife in his arms,
A baby at the bedside, safe in his cot.
I sweep past.

They have begun life anew, new love and a new life,
I am the old chapter,
My pages are read now.

It is two o'clock in the morning,
My house is silent now,
And I am driving home.

I joined a gym once, and resolved to go there at the crack of dawn three times a week. Predictably, this lasted for about a fortnight before I fell by the wayside. I can't now remember the gym at all, but I do remember that it was next door to a children's day-care centre. Between 7 and 7.30 a.m., the saddest procession of tired-eyed mums holding tiny, shawl-wrapped babies made their way inside. There was a kind of anguish about the scene. Economics made it necessary for the babies to be cared for by others, but none of the mums looked very happy about it.

7 a.m. Procession

Poor old babies, row on row,
In the daycare joint they go,
Strangers tend them, fill their tummies,
Tuck them in instead of mummies.

Snoring

We never did it much, but now we do it every night,
Married thirty years; in the end you get it right,
I don't mean to sound complacent but we do it
   more and more,
We clamber into bed and fall asleep, and then we snore.

Sometimes we snore in unison, sometimes we snore alone,
I'm a soprano snorer, and he's a baritone,
It never gets monotonous, each night a different sort,
Some finish with a gargle, others finish with a snort.

I only snore a bit but once I couldn't snore at all,
I suppose when I get going, you could hear me
   down the hall,
But my husband is remarkable, his snoring is so loud,
That beneath our bedroom window he's attracting
   quite a crowd.

It's true, he is phenomenal and sometimes when he snores,
My glass of water travels right across the chest of drawers,
And if he adds a flourish, like a splutter, shout or cough,
I've seen the glass of water jump a mile and topple off.

I could dance across the bedroom wearing just a feather boa,
He would still lay flat upon his back and snore like Krakatoa,
So let's hear it for the snorers now, wherever they may dwell,
Just lie back and enjoy; goodnight, sweet dreams my friends,
  sleep well.

Dosing the Dog

❧

I *was worried about my dog Ella. She had suddenly started to suffer from an itchy coat. All day long, underneath my desk, the dog scratched and fidgeted. I lathered her up with special shampoo from the vet but nothing seemed to calm the condition very much. I asked my friends on Twitter if anyone had any suggestions and a large number of helpful replies flooded in. Had I tried tea tree oil? Or tea tree shampoo? Had I tried a product called Stronghold? Or garlic tablets?*

I combed the internet and bought everything except the garlic tablets, thinking they sounded a bit unlikely. On researching the subject it made more sense, however. Apparently a dog which has eaten garlic gives off a slight smell, not noticeable to humans but highly repugnant to the microscopic parasites which burrow into the skin and cause irritation. Locating some tablets on the internet, I ordered a pot and within a few days the postman was walking up our path with it under his arm. I could smell him before he got to the door. The container was huge, and looking at the recommended dosage I could see why.

It said 'small dogs 2–5 tablets, medium dogs 5–10 tablets, large dogs 15–20 tablets'. Our dog is a large dog with a notoriously delicate digestion. That night, with her normal supper, I cautiously gave her just one garlic tablet.

Without wishing to sound tasteless or disgusting, or to describe an unpleasant scene too fully, the following morning it was all I could do to get the dog out of the back door before there was the most tremendous canine explosion. I looked at the terrible spectacle being enacted on our lawn and the one thought uppermost in my mind was: 'Thank God I didn't give her the other nineteen.'

My Little Grandson

Have you met my little grandson?
No, I didn't think you had,
Who's he like? Well some have said
He's rather like his Dad,
There are family resemblances
That people *claim* to see,
But anyone with half a brain …
Can see he looks like me.

My grandson's walking now
And he can nearly climb the fence!
But then, my father was athletic,
Ran in all the track events,
The *trophies* on his mantelpiece!
And some of them were whoppers,
Yes, my old dad could run like hell,
You ask the local coppers.

My grandson's very beautiful,
With gorgeous eyes that shine,
Cornflower blue, and frank and true,
Uncannily ... like mine,
He's absolute perfection,
See his photo on the shelf,
Each time I glance across,
It's just like looking at myself.

And though the old must fall away,
I see a vision clear,
At my grandson's great achievements,
I am sure that you will hear,
As he steps up for the Nobel Prize,
This genius of a man,
A voice beneath the daisies say:
'He gets it from his gran.'

Acknowledgements

Special thanks as always to my literary agent Vivien Green of Sheil Land for her support and encouragement over a very long period, to my editor Charlotte Cole for her good advice, to Susan Hellard for her matchless illustrations and to all at Ebury Press. Most particularly, I want to thank my terrific family for the happy environment in which I work.

Index of First Lines

P

Poor old babies, row on row, 151

S

See the hazel coppices, 138
See those ladies in the ring, 142
So your daughter's getting married! And your fine athletic son, 82

T

The days are slowly passing since I found her still and prone, 96
The lot of the insomniac, 105
The residents of Ilfracombe, 113
The seagull sits, like all his breed, 29
The swifts are back! 95
The wildlife in our garden, 67
There are conquering heroes, it's true, 134
There are rabbits and guinea pigs, fancy and plain, 17
They were soldiers, they met in the desert, 146
This is the final will and testament, 59

W

We are off for a treat, it's my birthday today, 47
We had our bedroom painted, it was rather tired and dated, 33
We never did it much, but now we do it every night, 152
Well done. You've made me late *again!* 14
What a boat race! What a crew! 31

Y

You have to dance while you are able, 147
You made it! I so hoped you'd call in on your way to town! 109

About the Author

Pam Ayres has been a writer, broadcaster and entertainer for almost forty years, since winning the TV talent show *Opportunity Knocks* in 1975. She is consistently one of the UK's top-selling female comedians with her theatre shows in the UK, and her poetry collections include *The Works*, *With These Hands* and *Surgically Enhanced*. Her books have sold millions over the years, and many of her poems are in school textbooks around the world including China, Australia, New Zealand, Holland, South Africa, the USA, Ireland and Singapore. Pam's autobiography of her years growing up in Berkshire during the post-war years, *The Necessary Aptitude*, was the UK's bestselling female autobiography in 2011. Pam is one of the few authors who has had bestsellers in the *Sunday Times* bestseller charts in almost every decade since the 1970s.

On BBC Radio 4, Pam has recorded four series of *Ayres on the Air*, with Series 5 scheduled for 2014. She has also appeared as a guest on programmes such as *Just A Minute*, *Loose Ends* and *Saturday Live*. Recent TV appearances include *My Life in Books*, *Paul O'Grady*, *The One Show*, *Gardeners' World*, *The Alan Titchmarsh Show* and *Countdown*. Pam has toured Australia and New Zealand regularly over the past thirty-five years, and is one of the few solo comediennes to have performed in the Concert Hall of the Sydney Opera House.

Pam has appeared three times before Her Majesty the Queen, and was awarded the MBE in the Queen's Birthday Honours of 2004. A keen and knowledgeable gardener, Pam and her husband have lived in Gloucestershire for over twenty-five years, where they have a smallholding with cattle, sheep, bees, chickens and guinea fowl.

You can follow Pam on Twitter at @PamAyres and her website is www.pamayres.com.